Septimus Winner

Musical Present for the Organ or Piano

Septimus Winner

Musical Present for the Organ or Piano

ISBN/EAN: 9783744768788

Printed in Europe, USA, Canada, Australia, Japan

Cover: Foto ©Thomas Meinert / pixelio.de

More available books at **www.hansebooks.com**

WINNER'S

MUSICAL PRESENT.

FOR THE

ORGAN OR PIANO.

SELECTED AND ARRANGED

BY

SEP. WINNER.

PHILADELPHIA:
J. M. STODDART & CO.
NEW YORK: DOUGLASS & MYERS. BOSTON: GEO. M. SMITH & CO.
SAN FRANCISCO, CAL.: A. L. BANCROFT & CO.
CHICAGO: J. S. GOODMAN.

CARD.

The constant and increasing demand for popular music at a reasonable rate which will adapt itself to the wants of the people has led the editor to collect in a convenient and cheap form the popular favorites which constitute this book.

With a view of meeting all tastes he has endeavored to make the collection comprehensive, embracing old favorites as well as new, arranging them so as to be equally available for the Organ or Piano.

He has made it his especial study to present such compositions as, whilst they please, will not tend to lower the standard of taste, with the hope that they may be of service in the study as well as the practice of music, affording entertainment and pleasure in the domestic pastime of the home circle.

THE EDITOR.

Entered according to Act of Congress, in the year 1874, by
J. M. STODDART & CO.,
In the Office of the Librarian of Congress, at Washington.

CONTENTS.

VOCAL.

	PAGE		PAGE
Agathe	8	Moet and Chandon	46
Beautiful Nell	40	Merry Heart	58
Do they Think of me at Home	52	Only be Kind	20
Dublin Bay	18	O ye Tears!	56
Dearest Spot of Earth to me	60	Paddle your own Canoe	48
Dear Little Shamrock	14	Robin Adair	6
Down the Quiet Valley	24	Speak to Me	20
Evening Song	62	Starry Night for a Ramble	36
Friends that we never Forget	12	Take Back the Heart	16
Good-bye at the Door	32	Touch the Harp Gently	42
Good-bye, Sweetheart	68	Three Fishers went Sailing	54
Heart Bowed Down	64	Then you'll Remember me	66
I cannot Sing the Old Songs	22	We're Nearing to the River Side	50
I've no Mother now I'm Weeping	30	When the Corn is Waving, Annie	34
Killarney	4	Won't you tell me Why, Robin	28
Katy's Letter	38	We Sat by the River	10
Little Maggie May	44	When the Swallows Homeward Fly	8
My Pretty Louise	42	You and I	10
My Blue-Eyed Nelly	26		

INSTRUMENTAL.

Attack Galop	72	L'Etoile Schottische	80
Blue Danube Waltz	70	Peri Waltzes	82
Black-key Polka Mazourka	92	Qui Vive Galop	84
Cecilia Grand March	98	Slumber Polka	76
Good-Luck March	74	Shadow Dance	86
German Polka	100	Storm Polka	94
Hit and Miss Galop	88	Sharpshooters' March	90
Jupiter Galop	96	Traumerei	102
Jolly Brothers Galop	78		

ROBIN ADAIR.

ROBIN ADAIR.

2 What made th' assembly shine?
    Robin Adair.
What made the ball so fine?
    Robin Adair.
What when the play was o'er,
What made my heart so sore,
What when the play was o'er?
Oh, it was parting with
    Robin Adair.

3 But now thou'rt far from me,
    Robin Adair.
But now I never see
    Robin Adair.
Yet him I loved so well,
Still in my heart shall dwell,
Yet him I loved so well,
Oh, I can ne'er forget
    Robin Adair.

AGATHE.

WHEN THE SWALLOWS HOMEWARD FLY.

English words by F. H. GORDON.   Music by FRANCIS ABT.

2 When the white swan southward roves,
There to seek the orange groves,
When the red tints of the west
Prove the sun has gone to rest;
In these words my bleeding heart
Would to thee its grief impart,
When I thus thy image lose,
Can I, ah! can I e'er know repose?

3 Hush! my heart, why thus complain?
Thou must too, thy woes contain;
Though on earth no more we rove
Loudly breathing vows of love;
Thou my heart must find relief,
Yielding to these words, belief:
I shall see thy form again,
Though to-day we part in pain.

WE SAT BY THE RIVER.
(YOU AND I.)

THE DEAR LITTLE SHAMROCK.

2

That dear little plant still grows in our land,
Fresh and fair as the daughters of Erin;
Whose smiles can bewitch and whose eyes can command,
In each climate they ever appear in.
For they shine thro' the bog, thro' brake, and the mireland,
Just like their own dear little Shamrock of Ireland,
The dear little Shamrock, the sweet little Shamrock,
The dear little, sweet little Shamrock of Ireland.

3

That dear little plant that springs from our soil,
When its three little leaves are extended;
Denotes from the stalk we together should toil,
And ourselves by ourselves be befriended.
And still thro' the bog, thro' the brake, and the mireland,
From one root should branch like the Shamrock of Ireland,
The dear little Shamrock, the sweet little Shamrock,
The dear little, sweet little Shamrock of Ireland.

DUBLIN BAY.

"I CANNOT SING THE OLD SONGS."

2 I cannot sing the old songs,
　Their charm is sad and deep,
　Their melodies would waken
　Old sorrows from their sleep,
　And though all unforgotten still,
　And sadly sweet they be,
|: I cannot sing the old songs,
　They are too dear to me. :|

3 I cannot sing the old songs,
　For visions come again,
　Of golden dreams departed,
　And years of weary pain;
　Perhaps when earthly fetters
　Have set my spirit free,
|: My voice may know the old songs
　For all eternity. :|

Let my grave be made 'neath the wildwood shade,
  Beside my darling Hallie;
Oh let me rest near the one loved best,
  Now sleeping in the valley:
For my joys have fled and my hopes are dead,
  My heart is sighing ever;
Since her smile is gone and I'm left alone,
  For our fate has been to sever.—CHORUS.

Wont You Tell Me Why, Robin?

BALLAD.

Composed and Arranged for the Piano-Forte.

By Claribel.

3 The other night we danced, Robin, beneath the hawthorn-tree,
I thought you'd surely come, Robin, if but to dance with me;
But Allan asked me first, and so I joined the dance with him,
But I was heavy-hearted, and my eyes with tears were dim,
And, oh, how very grave you looked, as once we passed you by,
Wont you tell me why, Robin? oh, wont you tell me why?

I'VE NO MOTHER, NOW I'M WEEPING.

Written and Composed

By T. Smith.

I'VE NO MOTHER, NOW I'M WEEPING.

2 Oh, how well do I remember, "take this little flow'r," said she,
  "And when with the dead I'm number'd, place it at my grave for me."
  f Dearest mother, I am sighing, on thy tomb I drop a tear;
  For the little plant is dying, now I feel so lonely here.—*Chorus.*

3 I've no mother, still I'm weeping, tears my furrow'd cheek now lave,
  Whilst a lonely watch I'm keeping, o'er her sad and silent grave;
  Soon I hope will be our meeting, then the gladness none can tell,
  Who for me will then be weeping, when I bid this world farewell?—*Chorus.*

THE GOOD-BY AT THE DOOR.

WHEN THE CORN IS WAVING, ANNIE DEAR.

WORDS AND MUSIC

BY CHARLES BLAMPHIN.

WHEN THE CORN IS WAVING, ANNIE DEAR.

A STARRY NIGHT FOR A RAMBLE.

(SONG AND CHORUS.)

SAMUEL BAGNALL.

1. I like a game at cro - quet, or bowl-ing on the green, I
2. I like to take my sweet - heart, "of course you would," said he, And
3. Tho' some will choose ve - lo - cipede, and o - thers take a drive, And

like a lit - tle boat - ing, to pull a - gainst the stream; But of
soft - ly whis - per in her ear: "how dear - ly I love thee;"...... And
some will sit and mope at home, half dead and half a - live;...... And

KATEY'S LETTER,

Composed for the Piano-Forte.

By Lady Dufferin.

2 I wrote it, and I folded it, and put a seal upon it;
'Twas a seal almost as big as the crown of my best bonnet;
For I would not have the Postmaster make his remarks upon it,
As I said inside the letter that I loved him faithfully.
    I love him faithfully,
And he knows it, oh, he knows it! without one word from me.

3 My heart was full, but when I wrote, I dared not put the half in.
The neighbors know I love him, and they're mighty fond of chaffing;
So I dared not write his name outside, for fear they would be laughing
So I wrote, "From little Kate to one whom she loves faithfully."
    I love him faithfully,
And he knows it, oh, he knows it! without one word from me.

4 Now, girls, would you believe it, that Postman, so consaited,
No answer will he bring me, so long as I have waited;
But maybe there mayn't be one for the raison that I stated,
That my love can neither read nor write, but he loves me faithfully.
    He loves me faithfully,
And I know where'er my love is, that he is true to me.

BEAUTIFUL NELL.

COMPOSED AND ARRANGED FOR THE PIANO-FORTE.

By R. Coote.

TOUCH THE HARP GENTLY.

Written by SAMUEL N. MITCHELL.   Composed by CHARLES BLAMPHIN.

LITTLE MAGGIE MAY.

Words by G. W. Moore.   Music by C. Blamphin.

44

2 White wines are pale and have no taste,
   The red indeed have too much hue,
Moselle in pleasing often fails,
   Still Hock's too slow and suits but **few**,
Lager is heavy and thick you know,
   Oh! I oh! I oh!
Water is dainty and free to **flow**,
   Oh! I oh! I oh!   *Chorus.*

3 Champagne's the wine for giving toasts,
   For headaches, and for waste of wealth;
But water pure is better far
   To quench the thirst or drink ones health.
Down on the banks where the lilies grow,
   Oh! I oh! oh! I oh!
Sparkling and bright do the streamlets flow,
   Oh! I oh! I oh!   *Chorus.*

WE'RE NEARING TO THE RIVER.

5 Dear Saviour, lead us safe along
   This waste of desert sand,
   Till we shall sing the victor's song,
   [:In the sweet Promised Land:]
   Sweet Promised Land.—Cho.

6 When earthly scenes shall disappear,
   Unite us with that band,
   Who bade farewell to loved ones here,
   [:To gain the Promised Land:]
   Sweet Promised Land.—Cho.

Do they think of me at Home?

POPULAR BALLAD.

MUSIC BY G. W. GLOVER.

2 Do they think of me at eve,—
   Of the songs I used to sing?
Is the harp I struck untouched,
   Does a stranger wake the string?
Will no kind, forgiving word,
   Come across the raging foam?
Shall I never cease to sigh,—
   Do they think of me at home?

3 Do they think of how I loved
   In my happy early days?
Do they think of him who came,
   But could never win their praise?
I am happy by his side,
   And from mine he'll never roam!
But my heart will sadly ask,—
   Do they think of me at home?

O YE TEARS!
SONG.

WORDS BY DR. MACKAY.   MUSIC BY FRANZ. ABT.

4. O ye tears! O ye tears! ye relieve me of my pain,
The barren rock of pride has been stricken once again;
Like the rock that Moses smote amid Horeb's burning sand,
It yields the flowing water, to make gladness in the land.
    O ye tears! O ye tears!

5. There is light upon my path! there is sunshine in my heart,
And the leaf and fruit of life shall not utterly depart;
Ye restore to me the freshness and the bloom of long ago,
O ye tears! O happy tears! I am thankful that ye flow.
    O ye tears! happy tears!

THE MERRY HEART.

Melody: The Guard on the Rhine, by Wilhelm.

ARRANGED FOR THE PIANO-FORTE.

By JEAN LOUIS.

THE DEAREST SPOT.

Composed and Arranged for the Piano-Forte.

By W. T. Wrighton.

EVENING SONG.

hills with ru - by's shin - ing, Then bids all the world good -
fold the shep - herds tend - ing, Home-ward hies the moun - tain

night! .... Good - night, good - night!
maid. .... Good - night, etc.

Good - night, good - night!

3 Bleaker winds the flowers benumbing;
  On the hearth the cricket sings;
  Home the laden bee flies humming,
  And the drowsy bat is coming,
    Darting on his leathern wings.
      Good-night!

4 Man now seeks his peaceful dwelling,
    Circles round the ruddy blaze,
  Of the sweets of labour telling,
  Till his heart with rapture swelling
    Grateful gives his Maker praise.
      Good-night!

HEART BOWED DOWN.

FROM THE OPERA OF THE

BOHEMIAN GIRL.

M. W. BALFE.

Then You'll Remember Me.

As sung in the Opera of the

Bohemian Girl.

Words by ALFRED BUNN, Esq.　　　　　　　Music by M. W. BALFE.

THEN YOU'LL REMEMBER ME.

"GOOD BYE, SWEETHEART, GOOD BYE."

JOHN L. HATTON.

BEAUTIFUL BLUE DANUBE WALTZ.

Arranged by SEP. WINNER.

BEAUTIFUL BLUE DANUBE WALTZ.

ATTACK GALOP.

F. ZIKOFF.

ATTACK GALOP.

GOOD LUCK MARCH.

Composed and Arranged for the Piano-Forte.

BY CARL FAUST.

GOOD LUCK MARCH.

SLUMBER POLKA.

By Beyer.

SLUMBER POLKA.

JOLLY BROTHERS.
GALOP.

FRANZ BUDIK.

JOLLY BROTHERS GALOP.

L'ETOILE SCHOTTISCH.

Peri Waltzes.

CHARLES D'ALBERT.

PERI WALTZES.

QUI VIVE GALOP.

QUI VIVE GALOP.

SHADOW DANCE.

HIT AND MISS GALOP.

ON HERVE'S COMIC OPERA.

L'ŒIL CREVE.

SHARP-SHOOTERS' MARCH.

COMPOSED FOR THE PIANO-FORTE.

By CARL FAUST.

SHARP-SHOOTERS' MARCH.

THE BLACK KEY POLKA MAZURKA.

COMPOSED FOR THE PIANO-FORTE.

By A. HERZOG.

THE BLACK KEY POLKA MAZURKA.

THE STORM POLKA.

JUPITER GALOP.

Composed and Arranged for the Piano-Forte.

By Charles Coote, Jr.

JUPITER GALOP.

CECELIA MARCH.

Composed and Arranged for the Piano-Forte.

By B. Bilse.

CECELIA MARCH.

GERMAN POLKA.

Composed and Arranged for the Piano-Forte.

By C. Faust.

GERMAN POLKA.

Traumerei Romanze.

B. SCHUMANN.

www.ingramcontent.com/pod-product-compliance
Lightning Source LLC
Chambersburg PA
CBHW020156170426
43199CB00010B/1072